BEAUTIFUL
HORSES
Amanda Neel

COLORING BOOK FOR ADULTS

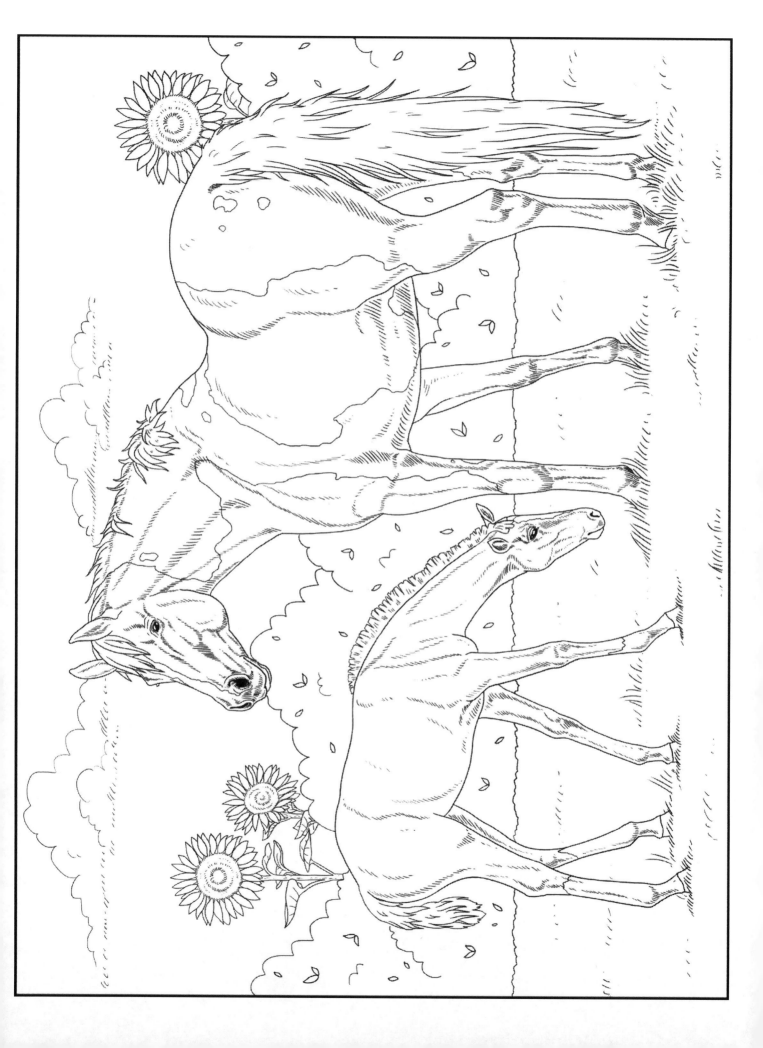

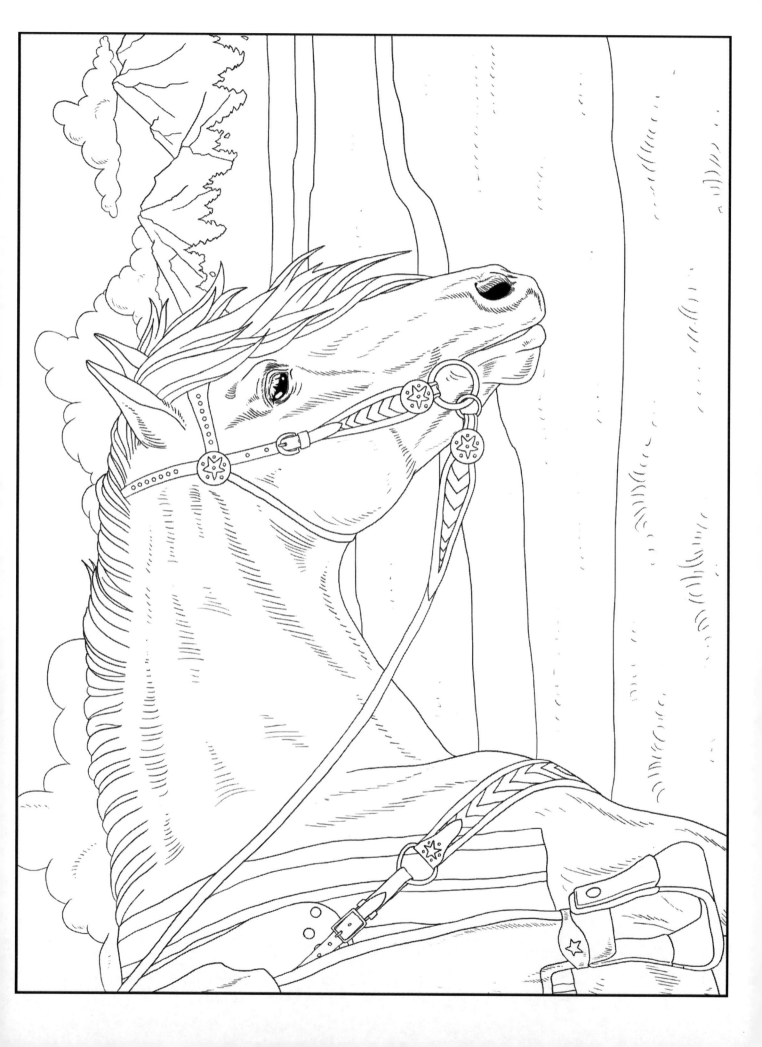

The following section includes all the previous images in a smaller version to allow you to test the colors and techniques before proceeding to work on the larger images.

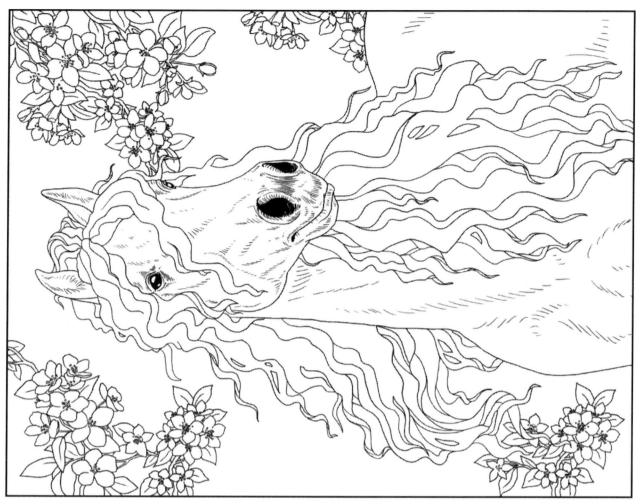

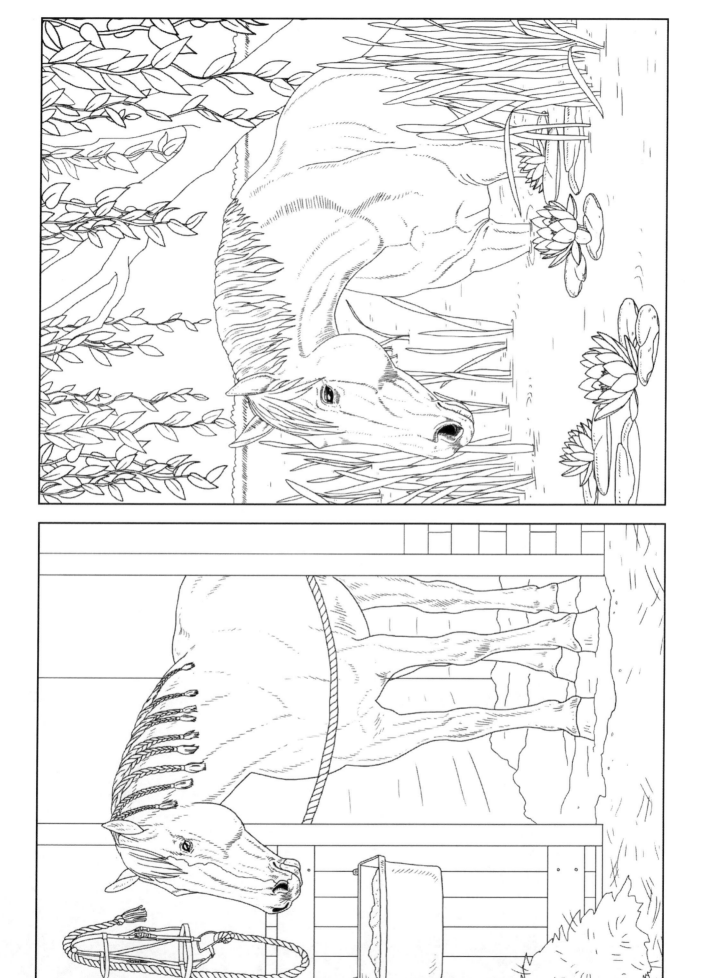

I love horses.

Many people feel the same attraction I have for horses and consider them the most highly esteemed and best-loved animals. This book contains a collection of 24 illustrations showing horses in a variety of scenes in the wild and in countryside settings. I hope you will enjoy this book and will get lots of positive emotions to color these images.

Happy Coloring!

Amanda Neel

About Amanda Neel

Amanda is an illustrator with a degree in Graphic Design. Her favorite subjects are related to nature. Her passion is to draw cats, dogs, horses and other animals.

ISBN-13: 978-1519277169

ISBN-10: 1519277164

We are always interested in hearing your thoughts and if you have enjoyed this book, please take a moment to post a review of the book on **Amazon.com**

Please feel free to contact us if you have any questions or comments: altispublishing@hotmail.com

From the same book series:

- Beautiful Mandalas: A Coloring Book Featuring 24 Artworks (Volume 1)
- Beautiful Mandalas: Inspire Your Creativity and Reduce Stress with Coloring Meditation (Volume 2)
- Happy Coloring: Geometric Kaleidoscopic Patterns (Volume 1)
- Happy Coloring: Flowers - Kaleidoscopic Patterns (Volume 2)
- Happy Coloring: Flower Patterns - Coloring Pages for Adults (Volume 3)
- Happy Coloring 4: Geometric Kaleidoscopic Patterns (Volume 4)
- Happy Coloring 5: Tropical Forest - Coloring Pages for Adults (Volume 5)
- Happy Coloring 6: Floral Patterns - Coloring Pages for Adults (Volume 6)
- Happy Coloring 7: Easy Patterns - Coloring Pages for Adults (Volume 7)
- Happy Coloring 8: Easy Patterns - Coloring Pages for Beginners (Volume 8)
- Happy Coloring 9: Intricate Patterns - Coloring Pages for Adults (Volume 9)
- Happy Coloring: Fantasy Forest - Wonderful Animals Coloring Book (Volume 10)
- Happy Coloring: Lovely Cats - Coloring Book for Adults
- Happy Coloring: Easy Flowers – Coloring Book for Adults

Visit our websites:

www.pinterest.com/happycoloring
www.facebook.com/happycoloringbooks
www.happycoloring.com

28777452R00048

Made in the USA
San Bernardino, CA
06 January 2016